Mexican Cookbook 2021

Bring To The Table The Authentic Taste And Flavors Of Mexican Cuisine Straight To Your Home Plus Tasty And Original Easy-To-Prepare Recipes

ALEXIS MORENO

Sommario

1. **ACAPULCO CHICKEN (EN ESCABECHE)**

2 cups	Unsalted chicken broth -- defatted
1 tablespoon	Olive oil
2 teaspoons	Ground cumin
2 tablespoons	Pickling spice
1/2	Red bell pepper -- sliced
1 pound	Boneless chicken breast -- halves
1/2	Yellow bell pepper -- sliced
2 tablespoons	Minced jalapeno chili with -- seeds
1	Onion, halved -- thinly sliced
1/3 cup	Rice wine vinegar

1/4 cup   Fresh cilantro leaves

3 large   Garlic cloves -- minced

baked (no oil) tortilla chips

Boil broth and pickling spice in heavy large saucepan ten minutes. Strain and return liquid to saucepan.Add chicken, onion, vinegar, garlic, oil and cumin to pan. Simmer over very low heat until chicken is just cooked through, about ten minutes. Transfer chicken and onions to shallow dish. Top with bell peppers and minced chilli. Boil cooking liquid until reduced to 2/3 c, about ten minutes. Pour liquid over chicken and let cool 30 minutes. Add cilantro tochicken mixture.Cover and refrigerate until well chilled, turning chicken occasionally, about 4 hours (can be prepared one day ahead). Slice chicken and transfer to plates. Top with marinated vegetables and some of the juices. Pass tortilla chips to use as "pushers." .

Makes 6 servings

2. **Almond Red Sauce**

1/2	cup	Slivered Almonds -- Toasted
1	cup	Onion -- Finely Chopped
1	each	Clove Garlic -- Crushed
2	tablespoons	Vegetable Oil
8	ounces	Tomato Sauce -- 1 cn
2	teaspoons	Paprika
1	teaspoon	Red Chiles -- Ground
1/4	teaspoon	Red Pepper -- Ground

Place almonds in food processor work bowl fitted with steel blade or in blender container; cover and process until finely ground. Cook onion and garlic in oil over medium heat, stirring frequently, until onion is tender. Stir

in remaining ingredients except almonds.

Heat to boiling; reduce heat. Simmer   1

minute   stirring   constantly;   stir   in

almonds.   Serve hot.

Makes about 1 3/4 cups of sauce.

3. **Basic Green Sauce**

1	cup	Onions; Chopped -- 2 Med.
1/2	cup	Vegetable Oil
10	ounces	Fresh Spinach -- Chopped
1/2	pound	Tomatillos -- Coarsely Chopped
4	ounces	Green Chiles; Chopped -- 1 cn
2	each	Cloves Garlic -- Crushed
1	tablespoon	Oregano Leaves -- Dried
1	cup	Chicken Broth
2	cups	Dairy Sour Cream

Cook and stir onions in oil in a 3-quart saucepan until tender. Stir in remaining ingredients except broth and sour cream. Cover and cook over medium heat for 5 minutes, stirring occasionally. Place mixture in food processor work bowl fitted with steel blade or in a blender container; cover and process until smooth, about 1 minute. Return mixture to saucepan; stir in broth. Heat to boiling; reduce heat.

Simmer uncovered for 10 minutes. Stir in sour cream.

Cover and refrigerate any remaining sauce. Makes about

4 cups of sauce.

4. **Basic Red Sauce**

8	each	Ancho Chilies
3 1/2	cups	Warm Water
1/2	cup	Onion -- Chopped
2	each	Garlic; Cloves -- chopped
1/4	cup	Vegetable Oil
8	ounces	Tomato Sauce -- 1 cn
1	tablespoon	Oregano Leaves -- Dried
1	tablespoon	Cumin Seed
1	teaspoon	Salt

Cover chiles with warm water. Let stand until softened, about 30 minutes; drain. Strain reserved liquid and the remaining ingredients. Heat ot boiling, reduce heat. Simmer, uncovered, 20 minutes; cool.Pour into a food processor work bowl fitted with steel blade or into a blender container; cover and process until smooth.

Cover and refrigerate up to 10 days. Makes about

2 1/2 cups sauce.

5. **Bean and Garlic Dip**

2	cups	Pinto Beans -- *
1/4 cup		Mayonnaise Or Salad Dressing
1	each	Clove Garlic -- Finely Chopped
1 1/2 teaspoons		Red Chiles -- Ground
1/4 teaspoon		Salt
		Pepper -- Dash of

*Pinto beans can be home cooked or canned. Mix all ingredients.Cover and refrigerate 1 hour. Serve with tortilla chips. Makes 2 cups of dip.

6. **BEANS COOKED IN A POT**

(FRIJOLES DE OLLA)

1	pound	Beans - black, turtle, pink -- or pinto
		An earthenware bean pot (I -- used my crock pot)
10	cups	Hot water
1/4	cup	White onion -- roughly sliced
2	tablespoons	Lard
1	tablespoon	Salt -- or to taste
2	large	Sprigs epazote (only if -- black beans are used

*Pinto or pink beans will need 12 to 14 cups water   Rinse the beans and run them

through your hands to make sure that
there are no small stones or bits of
earth among them.

Put the beans into the pot and cover them
with the hot water.

Add the onion and lard and bring to a boil.

As soon as the beans come to a boil,
lower the flame and let them barely
simmer, covered, for about 3 hours for
black beans and 2-1/2 hours for the
other varieties, or until they are
tender, but not soft. Do not stir during
this time.Add the salt and epazote, if
you are using it, and simmer for another
30 minutes. Set aside, preferably until the
next day.There should be plenty of soupy
liquid.

7. **Beef And Tequila Stew**

2	pounds	Meat -- *
	1/4 cup	Unbleached Flour
	1/4 cup	Vegetable Oil
	1/2 cup	Onion; Chopped -- 1 Medium
2	each	Bacon; Slices -- Cut Up
	1/4 cup	Carrot -- Chopped
	1/4 cup	Celery -- Chopped
	1/4 cup	Tequila
	3/4 cup	Tomato Juice
2	tablespoons	Cilantro; Fresh -- Snipped
1 1/2	teaspoons	Salt
15	ounces	Garbanzo Beans -- 1 Can
4	cups	Tomatoes; Chopped -- 4

Medium

2   each   Cloves Garlic -- Finely

Chopped

*   Meat should be beef boneless chuck,

tip or round, cut into 1-inch

Coat beef with flour. Heat oil in 10-

inch skillet until hot. Cook and stir

beef in oil over medium heat until

brown. Remove beef with slotted spoon

and drain.Cook and stir onion and bacon

in same skillet until bacon is crisp.

Stir   in   beef   and   remaining

ingredients. heat to boiling; reduce

heat.Cover and simmer until beef is

tender, about 1 hour.

8. **Beef Tacos**

1	pound	Ground beef
1	each	Chopped onion
		Salt to taste
1	each	Clove garlic (optional)
1	package	Taco shells
1	cup	Green chili or taco sauce

Saute' the beef and onion until brown. Salt to taste. Add garlic if desired. Place a heaping tablespoon of meat mixture in each shell and stuff with lettuce, tomato and cheese. Serve with the chili or taco sauce and top with sour cream or guacamole for an added treat.

9. **Bell Pepper Rajas**

1/2   each   Green Bell Pepper -- *

1/2   each   Red Bell Pepper -- *

1/2   each   Yellow Bell Pepper -- *

3/4   cup   Montery Jack Cheese --

Shredded

2   tablespoons

                           Chopped Ripe

Olives 1/4 teaspoon   Red   Pepper   --

Crushed

*   Peppers should be seeded and cut into 6

    strips

each. Cut bell pepper strips crosswise

into   halves. Arrange   in   ungreased

broilerproof pie pan, 9 X 1 1/4- inches

or round pan 9 X 2-inches. Sprinkle with

cheese, olives and red pepper.

Set oven control to broil. Broil peppers with tops 3 to

4 inches from heat until cheese is melted, about 3 minutes.

10. BLACK BEAN & SALMON APPETIZER

8		Corn tortillas
16 ounces	(1 cn)	Corn black beans -- rinsed and drained
7 ounces	(1 cn)	pink salmon; w bones -- drained
2 tablespoons		Safflower oil
1/4 cup		Fresh lime juice
1/4 cup		Fresh parsley -- chopped
1/2 teaspoon		Onion powder
1/2 teaspoon		Celery salt
3/4 teaspoon		Ground cumin
3/4 teaspoon		Garlic -- minced
1/2 teaspoon		Lime zest -- grated
1/4 teaspoon		Red pepper flakes -- dried

1/4 teaspoon   Chili pepper

Preheat oven to 350 degrees. Cut tortillas in triangles and toast oven until crisp, about 5 minutes. Combine the beans and salmon, flaking the salmon with a fork.Mix remaining ingredients; chill to blend flavors. Serve with tortilla chips.

11. Black Bean and Cheese Enchiladas

1	tablespoon	Vegetable oil
1/2 cup		Green onions -- sliced
1	teaspoon	Garlic -- minced
12	ounces	Canned tomatillos
4	ounces	Canned green chilies -- chopped
1/2 cup		Fresh cilantro -- chopped
1	tablespoon	Dried oregano
1	cup	Low-sodium chicken broth
12		Whole wheat tortillas -- 8"
15	ounces	Canned black beans
8	ounces	Fat-free Monterey Jack -- cheese, shredded, He

Heat oven to 350 F. To make sauce, cook green onions and garlic in oil until tender.   Add   tomatillos,

green chilies, cilantro and oregano.

Continue cooking until sauce comes to a

boil; reduce heat to low and continue

cooking about 10 minutes. Pour sauce into

blender container. Cover and blend on

high speed until smooth.

Return to saucepan and stir in chicken

broth.Cook

over medium heat about 15 minutes. Dip

each tortilla into sauce.Spoon

about 1 1/2 tb. black beans and 2 tb.

cheese onto each tortilla.Roll

tortilla around filling. Place seam side

down in 13" x 9" baking dish sprayed

with non- stick cooking spray. Pour

remaining sauce over tortillas; sprinkle

with remaining cheese.

Bake at 350 F for 20 to 25 minutes until cheese is melted and filling is hot. 12 Servings

12.**BLACK BEAN BURRITOS**

8 ounces   Black Beans; Dry* -- OR

30ounces   Black Beans -- Canned

1 medium   Onion -- Finely Chopped

2   Garlic Cloves -- Minced

1Jalapeno Pepper -- Seeded

And Chopped -- Up To Two

BeUsed Or To Taste

1teaspoon Chili Powder

1teaspoon Ground Cumin

5tablespoonsOlive Or Vegetable Oil

16uncesTomatoes; Cut Up -- 1 Can

11/4-Inch Thick Lemon Slice

1teaspoonDried Oregano --

Crushed 1/4 teaspoonSalt

1dashHot Pepper Sauce -- (Optional)

6Flour Tortillas

Salsa Guacamole

Chopped Tomato -- (Optional) Snipped Cilantro

Cook the dry beans*. Rinse and drain the cooked or canned beans and set aside.In a 4 1/2-quart Dutch oven, cook the onion, garlic, peppers, chili powder and cumin in hot oil, until tender, stirring occasionally. Stir in the drained beans, the UNDRAINED tomatoes, lemon, oregano, salt (omit if using the canned beans), and pepper sauce, if desired. Bring to boiling, reduce the heat, and simmer, uncovered, about 15 minutes or until thick.

Remove the lemon. In a blender container or food processor bowl, place one third of the mixture, cover, and blend until smooth. Repeat with the remaining beans.Return to the pan and heat through.In the meantime, wrap the tortillas in foil and warm in a 350 Degree F. oven for about 10 minutes.Place about 1/2 Cup of the bean mixture onto each tortilla. and fold the edges over to form a packet.Serve with salsa and guacamole If desired, top with chopped tomato and snipped cilantro.

TO COOK THE DRY BEANS:

To cook the dry beans in a 4 1/2-quart Dutch oven, combine the beans and enough water to cover.Bring to boiling then reduce the heat and simmer, uncovered, for2 minutes.Remove from the heat, cover, and let stand for 1 hour.(Or without cooking, soak the beans

vernight.) Drain the beans and rinse.

I

n the same Dutch oven combine the beans
and 5 cups of water or vegetable
broth.Bring to boiling, reduce the heat,
cover and simmer for 1 to 1 1/2 hours or
until tender.

13. BLACK BEAN NACHOS

FOR NACHOS:

Corn oil

2	Flour tortillas (8")
2	Chorizo or spicy sausage
1 cup	Black bean pesto
1 cup	Monterey jack cheese -- shred
2 tablespoons	Chopped cilantro (coriander)

FOR BLACK BEAN PESTO:

8 ounces	Dried black beans
1 quart	Water
1	Bay leaf
1	Ham hock
2	Jalapenos -- seeded
20milliliters	Garlic

Stems from 2 bunchs of

Cilantro (fresh coriander)

Salt/fresh ground pepper

For Black Bean Pesto:

Rinse and drain beans thoroughly. Place them in a large saucepan or soup kettle and add all remaining ingredients. Bring to a boil, reduce heat, simmer, uncovered, for 1 1/2 hours.

Remove and discard ham hock and bay leaf. Using slotted spoon, transfer bean mixture, in batches, to the bowl of a food processor. Process, adding cooking liquid as necessary to form a smooth, thick paste. You will use a total of about 1 cup liquid.

Transfer the pesto to a bowl and stir in

the salt and pepper if needed.

Refrigerate, covered, until ready to use.

Will keep in fridge for 2-3 days.

Yield:3 cups.

Nachos:

Preheat oven to 375F. Fill a heavy skillet with 1/2" corn oil. Heat it until oil just starts to move. Then fry the tortillas, one at a time, until light golden brown, about 15 seconds on each side. Drain on paper towels.

Slice chorizo into 1/4" thick rounds and saute them in a small skillet until crisp, about 5 minutes. Remove sausage from skillet and drain on paper towel.

Place tortillas on baking sheet, and spread pesto evenly over them.

Arrange sausage over pesto and

sprinkle with cheese. Top with chopped
cilantro.

Bake until brown, 20 minutes. Remove
from oven and cut each tortilla into
eight pieces. Serve immediately.

Makes 4 servings or 16 appetizers

14. BLACK BEAN QUESADILLAS

15	ounces	Can black beans -- drained
1/4	cup	Chopped tomato
3	tablespoons	Chopped cilantro
12	each	Black olives, pitted -- sliced
8	each	6" wholewheat tortillas
4	ounces	Soy cheese/jalapeno jack -- - shredded
32	each	Spinach leaves -- shredded
4	tablespoons	Hot salsa

Mash beans. Stir in tomato, cilantro & olives.

Spread evenly onto 4 tortillas. Sprinkle with cheese, spinach & salsa.

Top with remaining tortillas.

Preheat oven to 350F. Bake tortillas on ungreased cookie sheet for 12 minutes.Cut into wedges & serve.

15.**Black Bean Relish**

15	ounces	Black Beans; Canned -- *
3/4	cup	Tomato; Finely Chopped -- 1 med
1	each	Serrano Chile -- **
1/2	cup	Red Bell Pepper -- Chopped
1/4	cup	Red Onion -- Finely Chopped
2	tablespoons	White Wine Vinegar
1	tablespoon	Vegetable Oil
1/4	teaspoon	Salt

*   Black beans should be canned and they should be rinsed and drained.

** Serrano chile should be seeded and finely chopped.

Mix all ingredients. Cover and refrigerate until chilled, about 1 hour. Makes about 2 1/2 cups relish.

16. BLACK BEAN TORTILLA MELT

1	(15 oz) can black beans -- rinsed and drained
1/2 teaspoon	Chili powder
6	(6-inch) corn tortillas
1/4 cup	Minced fresh cilantro
1	Lime -- cut into six wedges
2	(4 oz) can chopped green -- chiles, undrained
3/4 cup	(3 oz) shredded cheddar -- cheese
	fresh or commercial salsa

Mash beans; add chili powder, stirring well. Spread about three tablespoons bean mixture on each tortilla. Sprinkle with cilantro, and squeeze 1 lime wedge over each. Top each tortilla with 2 tablespoons green chiles and 2 tablespoons

cheese.Bake tortillas at

450~ for 3 to

5 minutes or until cheese melts.Serve

with fresh salsa.

17.**Burrito**

Filling

4	tablespoons	Oil
12	ounces	Vegetable juice -- can
1 1/4 2	ounces	Beef broth -- can
3	each	Garlic clove -- minced
3 1/2	pounds	Beef stew meat
		Cheddar -- shredded
4	ounces	Chilies, green -- can

Brown meat in oil and drain. Add remaining ingredients except cheese. Simmer over low heat 2 to 3 hours. Shred meat with fork, drain excess liquid. Serve

on tortillas with cheese.

18.**Burritos Con Huevos**

1 1/2 pounds	flank steak -- * see note
1/2 teaspoon	black pepper
1/2 teaspoon	seasoned salt
2	cups	hot water
3		yellow onions
1		large bell pepper
1		jalapeno pepper -- chopped
2		tomatoes -- peeled and chopped
10		large eggs
2	cups	cheddar cheese -- shredded
8		flour tortillas

*   Use another cut of meat if flank steak is unavailable.

1.   To prepare steak, cut into 3-4 pieces and sprinkle with the salt

and pepper. Heat a very heavy pan with tight fitting lid. Add 1 tablespoon oil and brown the meat on each side.

2.   Add hot water and cover tightly. Simmer on low heat for 2 to 2- 1/2 hours or until meat shreds easily. Add more water during cooking if necessary. When meat is tender, shred into small bite-sized pieces.

3.   Cut the onions into thin slices and separate the slices into individual rings. Julienne the green pepper. Mince the jalapeno pepper (use a canned one if necessary).

4.   In a large heavy skillet, heat 2 tablespoons oil; add the onions and green peppers.

Saute until onions are translucent and limp. Add the chopped fresh tomato and the minced jalapeno and continue cooking for

3 minutes more.

5.	Add the shredded meat, 10 eggs which have been lightly beaten, and the shredded cheese. Proceed as though you were scrambling eggs.

6.	Warm the flour tortillas while cooking the filling, or quickly run each tortilla over the flame on a gas stove, just to soften. Fill each tortilla with 1/8th of the mixture. Roll the tortillas by turning one side up and folding the edges inward. Wrap the lower third in foil or waxed paper and serve immediately.

Serving Ideas : Serve with sour cream and avocado.

19. CABRITO AL PASTOR (BROILED KID)

2   ids [baby goats] --

                          6 1/2 to

-8 1/2 lbs each

3   tablespoons Salt

1   cup   Mild vinegar

          For the

garnish:

2   cups   Guacamole (recipe

-separately)

3   tablespoons White   onion   --

          chopped

1   cup   Tomato   --   finely

chopped

3   tablespoons Cilantro --   finely

chopped

3   tablespoons Chiles serranos --

finely

-chopped

1   Recipe Frijoles de

Olla

-mashed (recipe separately)

1 1/2 cups   Mozzarella OR Monterey Jack

-cheese -- freshly grated

16   Totopos   (crisply

fried

-tortilla wedges)

For the kid:

Put kids in a large stockpot, and cover

with water.A

dd salt and vinegar.

Set aside for 2 hours. Meanwhile,

build a pile of mesquite wood on the

ground, and burn down to white coals.

Remove kids from water and thread on spits.

Arrange over the hot coals, and roast for 2 to 3 hours, depending on the kids' weight, basting occasionally with a little salted water. Turn spits continuously so that the meat cooks evenly, or use a rotisserie. Add more white coals if necessary.

To serve, cut kid in pieces, and place on plates.Garnis with guacamole, onion, tomato, cilatro, and chiles.ervewithj Frijoles de Olla sprinkled with cheese, totopos, and Pico de Gallo sauce. The kid may be shredded and used in fried tacos.

20.**Calabacitas**

4	each	Zucchini or yellow squash
1	each	Sliced
1	each	Large onion -- chopped
3	tablespoons	Oil
2	each	Cloves garlic minced
4	ounces	Can chopped green chili
16	ounces	Can whole kernel corn
1/4	teaspoon	Garlic salt or
1	cup	Grated cheddar cheese

Saute' squash and onion in oil until barely tender. Add garlic salt (or fresh garlic), chilies, corn and cheese; mix well. Put in buttered 1- quart casserole and bake at 400 for 20 minutes.

21.California Chilled Salsa

2	cups	tomatoes -- peeled, chopped
1		celery stalk
1		onion -- diced
1		green pepper -- diced
1	teaspoons	salt
1/2		
1	tablespoon	cider vinegar
1	tablespoon	sugar
1		green chili peppers -- chopped

* Also delicious made with red sweet peppers or a combination of red and green for nice color.

Combine all ingredients; if finer

texture is desired may be put through food grinder using fine blade. Cover tightly and chill vernight.

Serving Ideas : Serve cold as a relish with meat.

22.Caramelized Carnitas

1 1/2 pounds		Pork Shoulder; Boneless -- *
2	tablespoons	Brown Sugar -- Packed
1	tablespoon	Tequila
1	tablespoon	Molasses
1/2 teaspoon		Salt
1/4 teaspoon		Pepper
2	each	Clove Garlic -- Finely Chopped
1/3 cup		Water
1	each	Green Onion w/top -- Sliced

*   Pork should be cut up into 1-inch cubes.

Place pork cubes in single layer in 10-inch skillet. Top with remaining ingredients except green onion. Heat to boiling; reduce heat.

Simmer uncovered, stirring occasionally

until the water has evaporated and the pork is slightly caramelized, about 35 minutes.

Sprinkle with green onion and serve with wooden picks.

23. Carne Adovada (Marinated Pork)

4	pounds	Pork(ribs -- chops or other)
2	teaspoons	Salt
3	each	Garlic cloves -- crushed
2	teaspoons	Whole leaf oregano
1	quart	Blended red chili sauce

Sprinkle meat with salt. Add garlic and oregano to blended chili. Pour over meat and marinate in refrigerator 6-8 hours or overnight. Cook slowly on top of stove or in 350 oven until meat is done, about 1 hour. Thick slices of potatoes may be marinated with the meat.

24. CARNE ASADA

| 1 1/2 | pounds | Top Round Steak Or Boneless |
| | | Chuck Steak, |

MARINADE

1/4	cup	Red Wine Vinegar
2	tablespoons	Oil
1	teaspoon	Sage Leaves
1	teaspoon	Summer Savory
1/2	teaspoon	Salt
1/2	teaspoon	Dry Mustard
1/2	teaspoon	Paprika

-----BASTING SAUCE-----

2	tablespoons	Steak Sauce
12		Flour Tortillas -- 5 to 8
		Inches In Diameter
2	medium	Onions -- Sliced Paper Thin Or

Chopped

4   ounces   Whole Green Chilies -- Cut

Into Strips

Softened Butter Or Margarine

Salsa

Guacamole

Place steak in plastic bag or non-metal baking dish.

In   small bowl, combine marinade ingredients. Pour over steak, turning to coat. Seal bag or cover dish; marinate at least 6 hours or overnight in refrigerator, turning once or twice.

When ready to barbecue, drain meat, reserving marinade by placing in small saucepan. Add steak sauce to marinade;

blend well. Heat on grill.

Place steak 4 to 6 inches from medium-hot coals.Cook

30 to 40 minutes, turning once, or until desired doneness, brushing occasionally with marinade. Meanwhile, heat foil-wrapped tortillas on grill until thoroughly heated and steaming, wrap in cloth napkin or towel to keep warm.

To serve, cut steak across grain into thin slices.Spoon any remaining marinade over slices.Arrange steak, warmed tortillas, onions, chilies, butter, salsa and guacamole on a large platter.Spread butter on tortilla; top with meat and any combination of vegetables or sauce. Roll up to eat.

Note: Be sure to heat basting sauce thoroughly to ensure safety for use as a sauce at the table.

25. CARNE ASADO (MEXICAN STYLE

BEEF TIPS & GRAVY)

1	pound	Beef stew meat
4		Cloves garlic -- chopped
1		Onion -- grated
1	teaspoon	Cumin -- ground
1	teaspoon	Black pepper -- ground
2	cans	Tomato sauce (or 1 large)
		Granule style beef bouillon
		Flour

Sort through stew meat trimming excess fat, gristle. Cut into 1" pcs. if necessary. In med. size, heavy bottom pot, place enough bacon drippings or melted lard to cover bottom. Place stew meat, garlic and onion in pot and saute

untill meat is lightly browned. Add water

to cover and two or three tbs. beef

bouillon, cumin, pepper and tomato sauce.

Cover.

Simmer on low heat until meat is tender.

Toward end of cooking time (abt. 1 hr.)

add flour to thicken and continue

simmering , stirring from time to time,

additional 10 min.

Re

move from heat and serve with spanish

rice (Sopa de Arroz) and refried beans.

Sa

lsa cruda,

Pico de Gallo are good garnishes.

Coarsely chopped lettuce and tomatoes

and shredded cheddar cheese. Serve with
warm flour tortillas, or make soft
tacos.

26.Carne   Gisada   Con   Papas

(Meat & Potatoes)

3	pounds	Round Steak -- 1/2" Thick
2	pounds	Potatoes
8	ounces	Tomato Sauce
1	1/2 teaspoons	Salt
	1/2 teaspoon	Ground Pepper
	1/2 teaspoon	Ground Cumin
1	each	Large Clove Garlic -- Smashed
		Water

Cut round steak into cubes and brown in shortening in heavy skillet or Dutch oven.Peel and cube potatoes (approximately in 1/2-inch cubes).

Once meat is slight browned add

potatoes and continue to brown. (Don't worry if it sticks to the bottom of the skillet.   Add   tomato   sauce,   salt, pepper, cumin powder and garlic.

Add Approcimately ONE cup of water and simmer until meat and potatoes are   tender.   Potatoes   will   thicken sauce.

27.**Carne Guisada**

3	pounds	round steak, trimmed -- cubed
2	tbsps	vegetable oil
1	tbsp	flour
2	tbsps	chopped
2	tbsps	chopped green pepper
2	tbsps	chopped tomato
1	to 2	cloves garlic -- minced
10	ounce can	tomatoes and green chiles -- undrained
8	ounce can	tomato sauce
1/4	cup	water
1	1 1/2 tsps	ground cumin
		Salt and pepper -- to taste

Cook steak in oil in a heavy skillet over

medium-high heat, stirring constantly, until browned. Sprinkle with flour and stir well. Add onion and remaining ingredients. Bring to a boil over medium hear; reduce heat and simmer, uncovered, 40 minutes or until meat is tender and sauce is thick.

Serve in flour tortillas or over hot cooked rice.

28.Casera Sauce

1 1/2 cups	Tomatoes -- Finely Chopped
1/2 cup	Onion -- Chopped
1 each	Clove Garlic -- Finely Chopped
1 each	Jalapeno Chile; Canned -- *
1/2 teaspoon	Jalepeno Chile Liquid
1 tablespoon	Cilantro; Fresh -- Snipped Fine
1 tablespoon	Lemon Juice
1/2 teaspoon	Oregano Leaves -- Dried
1 1/2 teaspoons	Vegetable Oil

*   Jalapeno Chile should be seeded and finely chopped. Mix all ingredients in glass or plastic bowl.Cover and refrigerate up to 7 days. Makes about 2

29. **CHALUPA**

1	pound	Pinto beans
3	pounds	Pork roast
7	cups	Water
1/2	cup	Onion -- chopped
2		Garlic cloves -- minced
1	tablespoon	Salt
2	tablespoons	Chili powder
1	tablespoon	Cumin
1	teaspoon	Oregano
4	ounces	Green chili peppers -- chopped (one can)

Put all ingredients in a dutch oven, an electric crockery cooker, or a heavy kettle. Cover and simmer about 5 hours, or until the roast falls apart and the beans are done. Uncover and cook about 1/2 hour, until the desired thickness is achieved.

30.**Cheesy Chilanda Casserole**

1	pound	Ground Beef
1	each	Med. Bell Pepper -- chopped
1	each	Clove Garlic -- minced
16	ounces	Pinto Beans -- drained
15	ounces	Tomato Sauce
1	cup	Picante Sauce -- med. hot
1	teaspoon	Ground Cumin
1/2	teaspoon	Salt
12	each	Corn Tortillas
2	cups	Shredded Cheese
		Lettuce -- shredded
		Sour Cream
		Fresh Tomato -- chopped

*   Cheese may be Monterey Jack or

Cheddar Brown meat with pepper, onion and garlic; drain. Add beans, tomato sauce, picante sauce, cumin and salt.

Simmer 15 minutes. Spoon small amount of meat mixture in 13x9 baking dish.

Top with 6 tortillas. Top with half the remaining meat mixture; sprinkle with cheese, repeat (except for cheese).

Cover tightly with aluminum foil.

Bake at 350" for 20 minutes. Remove foil and top with remaining cheese. Bake uncovered for 5 minutes. Top with lettuce, tomato, sour cream and additional picante sauce.

31. HEESY ONION ROLL-UPS

1	cup	(8 oz.) sour cream
8		ounces Pkg. cream cheese -
-	1/2	cup Finely shredded cheddar -
softened		

- cheese

3/4	cup	Sliced green onions
1	tablespoon	Lime juice
1	tablespoon	Minced seeded jalapeno --

pepper

10	ounces	Pkg. flour tortillas (6"
		--

size)

"These roll-ups are very fast to fix

and you can make them ahead and keep

them wrapped in the refrigerator until you're ready to serve." -

Picante sauce

Combine the first six ingredients in a bowl; mix well. Spread on one side of tortillas and roll up tightly.Wrap and refrigerate for at least 1 hour.Slice into 1" pieces. Serve with picante sauce.Yields:

About 5 dozen

32. CHICKEN ACAPULCO WITH

CREAMY SHRIMP SAUCE

4 large	Poblano peppers
1/4 cup	Onion -- chopped
1/2 pound	Medium shrimp -- lightly
	Cooked, peeled -- and chopped
1/4 cup	Cilantro -- chopped
1/4 pound	Monterey jack cheese
	Shredded
2	8 ozs chicken breasts
	Halved, deboned -- and
	Pounded flat
2 teaspoons	White pepper
	Salt -- to taste
12	6-in long strings
	Oil -- for frying

-----CREAMY SHRIMP SAUCE-----

3	Shallots -- diced
1 cup	White wine
1/2 cup	Fish stock or chicken broth
1 pound	Small shrimp
2 cups	Whipping cream
3/4 pound	Butter

ROAST PEPPERS: Place poblano peppers under the broiler and char on all sides. Put in plastic bag and freeze 10 minutes. Remove from freezer, rub off peel, then slit to remove seeds under running water.

Preheat oven to 400 degrees F. In a medium saute pan, saute onion, shrimp, and cilantro until the shrimp are almost cooked, about 5 minutes. Place in mixture in a bowl, add the cheese and set aside.

TO ASSEMBLE: Lay the four prepared chicken breasts flat, skin-side down. Season with salt and white pepper.

Layer each breast with one pepper and 2 to 3 tablespoons shrimp/cheese mixture over pepper.

Roll each breast tightly to form a cylinder. Tie each cylinder in 3 places, both ends and in the middle.

In a skillet, heat about 1/4-inch of oil. Lightly brown chicken breasts, one at a time, on all sides. Remove from heat, transfer to a oven-proof dish and bake for 10 minutes until golden brown.

Remove from oven. Cut strings and slice chicken into 1-inch roulades (rounds).

Drizzle a few tablespoons of Creamy Shrimp Sauce onto a plate and arrange the roulades on top of the sauce. Serve warm. Makes 4 servings.

TO MAKE CREAMY SHRIMP SAUCE: In a saucepan over medium- high heat, combine shallots and wine. Cook until reduced by three-fourths. Add stock/broth and shrimp and cook until reduced by half. Add the cream and reduce again by half. Whisk in the butter by tablespoons. Cook until butter melts and sauce is well-blended. Remove from heat. Recipe:

33. CHICKEN ALEJANDRO

1/2 cup	Onions -- thinnly sliced
1	Garlic clove -- minced
1 tablespoon	Margarine or butter
1 cup	Medium salsa
1/2 teaspoon	Sugar
1/4 teaspoon	Cinnamon
1/8 teaspoon	Cloves -- ground
1/2	Bay leaf
4	Chicken breast halves -- boneless
2 teaspoons	Cornstarch
8 ounces	Tomato sauce
1 small	Orange; peeled -- sections
	Rice

In a large skillet, over medium heat,

cook onion and garlic in margarine until tender. Stir in salsa, sugar, cinnamon, cloves, and bay leaf; add chicken. Cover and simmer for 30 minutes. Remove chicken to heated platter; keep warm. In a small bowl, dissolve cornstarch in tomato sauce; stir into skillet. Cook, stirring constantly until the mix thickens and begins to boil. Add orange sections; heat through.

Discard bay leaf. Serve chicken over rice with the sauce over all.

34. CHICKEN ALMENDRADO

1/2	cup	Onion; Chopped -- 1 Medium
2	tablespoons	Margarine Or Butter
1	tablespoon	Vegetable Oil
1	cup	Chicken Broth
1/4	cup	Almonds -- Slivered
1	tablespoon	Red Chiles -- Ground
1	teaspoon	Vinegar
1/2	teaspoon	Sugar
1/2	teaspoon	Cinnamon -- Ground
4	each	Chicken Breast Halves -- *
		Almonds -- Slivered

Chicken Breasts Halves should be
boneless. Cook and stir onion in
margarine and oil in a 10-inch skillet,
until tender. Stir in broth, 1/4 cup of

almonds, the ground red chiles, vinegar, sugar and cinnamon. Heat to boiling; reduce the heat and simmer, uncovered, for 10 minutes. Spoon mixture into a blender container, cover and blend on low speed until smooth, about 1 minute.Return sauce to skillet.

Dip chicken breasts into the sauce to coat both sides.Place skin sides up in a single layer in the skillet.Heat to boiling and then reduce the heat, cover and simmer until done, about 45 minutes.Serve sauce over chicken and sprinkle with the remaining slivered almonds.

35.CHICKEN BREASTS OLE'

3	Whole chicken breasts -- boneless & split
4ounces	Green chilies -- diced
3/4 cup	Cheddar cheese -- shredded Monterey
3/4 cup	Jack cheese -- shredded
3tablespoons	Onion -- finely chopped
1/3 cup	1/4 Butter -- melted Chili
teaspoon	1/4 powder Cumin -
teaspoon	- ground
cup	Tortilla chips -- crushed

1

Wooden toothpicks

Remove skin from chicken. Between sheets of waxed paper, pound each until 1/4" thick. Drain chilies and combine with the cheeses and onion. Divide into 6 equal portions. Sprinkle one portion down center of each breast.

Roll chicken around filling, folding in ends and securing with wooden toothpicks. Combine the butter, chili powder and cumin. Coat rolls with butter mixture and roll in chips.

Arrange chicken, seam side down, in a shallow greased casserole. Bake at 375 degrees for 45 minutes. Serve with sour cream and taco sauce. Goes great with Mexican rice.

36.CHICKEN BREASTS

SOUTHWESTERN

2/3	cup	Vegetable oil
1/3	cup	Lime juice
2	tablespoons	Green chilies -- chopped
1	teaspoon	Fresh garlic -- minced
4		Chicken breasts halves --

Skinned

| 8 | slices | Cheddar cheese Salsa |

In 9" square baking pan stir together all marinade ingredients. Add chicken breasts; marinate, turning once, in refrigerator at least 45 minutes. Meanwhile, prepare grill placing coals to one side; heat until coals are ash white. Make aluminum foil drip pan;

place opposite coals. Remove chicken from marinade; drain.

Grill chicken 7 minutes; turn.

Continue grilling until fork tender, 6 to 8 minutes. Top each chicken breast with 2 slices cheese. Continue grilling until cheese begins to melt. Serve with salsa.

37. CHICKEN BREASTS WITH

CHILIES AND ARROZ BLANCO

8	Chicken breast halves -- skinned and boned Salt and freshly ground -- black pepper
4 tablespoons	Butter or margarine -- divided
2 tablespoons	Vegetable oil
1 large	Onion -- thinly sliced and into rings
2 pounds	Anaheim chilies -- peeled and divided or 4
	Cans (4 oz each) green -- chilies, drained
1 cup	Milk -- divided

2 tablespoons Flour

2 cups   Sour cream

1   4 oz cup grated Cheddar --

              cheese

Season chicken with salt and pepper. In large skillet, heat 2 Tbsp butter and oil. Add chicken and cook over medium high heat until light brown on both sides.

Remove from pan and set aside. Cook onion in skillet until soft, but not brown. Cut all but 3 chilies into strips. Add strips to onion and cook over medium heat 5 minutes.

Remove from heat and set aside. Place 3 whole chilies,

1/4 cup milk and 1/2 tsp salt in

blender or food processor. Process
until smooth.

Add sour cream and blend a few seconds
more. Set aside. Melt remaining
2 Tbsp butter in small saucepan. Blend
in flour. Add 3/4 cup milk and cook,
stirring until smooth and thickened.
Remove from heat. Stir in sour cream
mixture. Arrange half the chicken
breasts in a casserole. Top with half
the onion chilies mixture. Spread with
half the sauce. Repeat layers. Bake,
covered, @ 375 degrees for 25 minutes.
Remove from oven. Sprinkle with
cheese. Bake 3 to 4 minutes. Serve
over beds of fluffy Arroz Blanco.
Makes 6 servings.

ARROZ BLANCO: Melt 2 Tbsp butter or margarine in 2 to 3 quart saucepan. Add 1 cup uncooked rice and cook over moderate heat until golden, stirring often. Add 1/2 cup chopped onions and 2 cloves minced garlic; cook until

onions are soft but not brown. Add 2 cups chicken broth and

1 tsp cumin seed. Bring to a boil; stir once or twice. Reduce heat, cover, and simmer 15 minutes or until rice is tender and liquid is adsorbed. Salt to taste.

38.**Chicken Chilaquiles**

4		Chicken Breast Halves Without Skin -- boned
1/2 Tsp	Cumin
	Salt And Pepper -- to taste
8 Oz	Tortilla Chips -- Lightly Salted
28 Oz	Green Enchilada Sauce
8 Oz	Monterey Jack Cheese -- shredded
1/2 Cup	Cilantro -- chopped
4	Green Onions -- chopped
8 Tbsp	Light Sour Cream -- or real sour cream
1/2 Cup	Salsa Fresca -- fresh or storebought

Sprinkle breasts with cumin, salt and pepper. Broil until just done. I do this in a toaster oven for about 5 minutes per side. Slice or shred chicken.

Evenly cover four microwave safe dinner plates with tortilla chips. Sprinkle with chicken.Pour enchilada sauce over the chicken and then microwave each plate for 1 to 1-1/2 minutes. Top with cheese and microwave each plate for 45-60 seconds or until cheese melts in the center of plate.

Meanwhile, chop and combine cilantro and green onions.Spinkle a 1/4 cup mixture over each of the heated plates.Put a dollop of sour cream in the center of each plate and surround with salsa fresca.

39.**Chicken Enchiladas — Lowfat**

10ounces   Cooked chicken -- shredded

           2 cups

           Scallions -- finely chopped

2 1/2 cups   Enchilada sauce -- see recipe

           6-inch prepared corn -- tortillas;

1 1/2   Part-skim   mozzarella   cheese   --

     ounce   grated

   s

Preheat oven to 400F, unless you have a microwave. In a bowl, combine the chicken, half the scallions, and 1/2 cup of the enchilada sauce. Soften the corn tortillas, two at a time, by steaming them for 10 seconds, or cook in a microwave for 10 second on high.

Spoon 1 cup of the enchilada sauce on the bottom of a 9x11-inch pan. Fill each tortilla with about 1/4 cup of the chicken mixture. Roll each tortilla and place seam side down on the sauce in the pan. Top with the remaining cup of enchilada sauce, sprinkle with the cheese and the remaining scallions. Bake for 10 minutes or microwave on high for 5 minutes. YIELD: Serves 8

40. CHICKEN ENCHILADAS WITH

PASILLA CHILI SAUCE

2	tablespoons	Peanut oil
1		2-oz. package dried pasilla Chilies, stemmed, seeded Torn into 1-inch pieces
	1/2 cup	Whole blanched almonds Chopped
4		Chicken breast halves
6	cups	Chicken stock or canned Low-salt broth
	1/2 teaspoon	Cumin seeds
4		Plum tomatoes, cored Quartered
	1/2	Onion -- quartered

4		Cloves garlic -- peeled
2	tablespoons	Firmly packed golden brown Sugar
1	teaspoon	Coarse salt
		Peanut oil (for deep frying)
16		Corn tortillas
2 1/2 cups		Grated Montery Jack Cheese
1	cup	Creme fraiche or sour cream
1		Avocado, peeled, seeded Sliced
		Fresh cilantro sprigs

Heat 2 tablespoons oil in large pot over high heat. Add chilies and almonds.Saute until chilies darken and almonds are golden, about 2 minutes.Using slotted spoon, transfer chilies and almonds to bowl. Reduce heat to medium.Season chicken with salt and pepper. Add to same pot and brown on all sides, about 5 minutes. Add stock; simmer until chicken is cooked through, aobut 20 minutes. Transfer chicken to another bowl using slotted spoon; cool.Reserve stock in pot.

Toast cumin seeds in heavy small skillet over medium- low heat until aromatic, about 1 minute.Mince cumin seeds. Add cumin, chili mixture, tomatoes, quartered onion, garlic, sugar and salt to stock. Simmer until all ingredients are very soft, about 45 minutes.

Working in batches, puree stock mixture
in blender. Return to pot. Boil until
reduced to 4 cups, stirring

occasionally, about 20 minutes.

Season with salt and pepper. (Can be
made 1 day ahead. Chill chicken and
sauce separately.)

Remove skin from chicken and discard.Cut
meat from bones and shred. Transfer to
bowl and combine with 1/2 cup sauce. Set
filling aside.

Oil two 139-inch glass baking
dishes.Pour oil into deep skillet to
depth of 1/2 inch and heat to 375-
degree F. Fry tortillas 1 at a time
until softened, about 5 seconds per

side.Using metal sapatula, transfer to paper towels.Spread 1 tablespoon sauce over each tortilla. Sprinkle each with 2 tablespoons cheese and 1 tablespoon chopped onion. Place 1/3 cup chicken down center of each tortilla; roll up. Place seam side down in baking dishes. (Can be made 1 hour ahead.

Cover.)

Preheat oven to 350-degree F. Pour remaining sauce over enchiladas. Sprinkle with remaining cheese. Bake until heated through, about 20 minutes. Top with creme fraiche, avodado and clinatro.

CPSIA information can be obtained
at www.ICGtesting.com
Printed in the USA
BVHW041355200421
605393BV00001B/234